REIMAGINED
Moments

JACINTA HUDSON

Copyright © August 2022 Jacinta Hudson

All rights reserved. No part of this book may be reproduced without the written consent of the copyright holder except in the case of quotations for a book review.

Cover Design by Stone Ridge Books

ISBN: 978-0-6489289-6-6

To teenage Jacinta

I am who I am because you were brave enough to be you.

That's not an easy thing to do at any age, so I will never stop being grateful for your strength through your hardest times, and the bravery you showed in sharing those times with the world.

Thank you for always dreaming bigger and showing others that they can dream as big as they like and be exactly who they are.

This one's for you, Beautiful.

CONTENTS

THE POEMS …………………………………….………..7

BONUS POEMS…………………………………..……..107
(Adults Only)

INTERVIEW WITH THE AUTHOR………………..……..121
with Alex Clifford

THEN & NOW……………………………………………....137
Behind the Scenes of Just a Thought – Reimagined Moments

ACKNOWLEDGEMENTS…………………………………..145

ABOUT THE AUTHOR………………………………...…….147

Open your mind and close your eyes.
Sit and think with me.
Open your eyes. I wear no disguise.
Tell me what you see.
So much to learn in such a world.
And one so big and new.
Just stick with me and then you'll see.
That all I want is you.

Although my eyes can't see you.
I know that you are there.
Although my nose can't smell you.
I know that you are there.
Although my ears can't hear you.
I know that you are there.
Although my hands can't touch you.
I know that you are there.

Although your eyes can't see me.
Imagine I am there.
Although your nose can't smell me.
Spray perfume through the air.
Although your ears can't hear me.
My voice is everywhere.
Although your hands can't touch me.
Feeling with your heart, you care.

REIMAGINED MOMENTS

༄༅

Fairy floss is sweet. But the memory of you is sweeter.
I've been so lost without you. On the edge of sanity, I teeter.
In the time we spent together, I took my cues from you.
I've floundered without you in my life, unsure just what to do.

I'm here left without you because you went away.
You've flown off without me because I had to stay.
I wish you didn't have to go. I rather wish you'd stayed.
But life was rough and short for you. Numbered were your days.

But even though I grieve you and wish that you were here.
You need to know that I'm okay. There's nothing you should fear.
I've become a strong woman. And I credit you for all my joy.
You taught me the beauty in the hard times, and the importance of cuddling stuffed toys.

❦

You're bringing home the bacon.
And you're eating all the pie.
If *you* won't clean the mess up.
Then *you'll* live in the sty!

❦

Times pass so kiss my ass.
Because I want you no more.
Times come so kiss my bum.
You're not my type, I'm sure.

REIMAGINED MOMENTS

❧

I'm Jacinta.
I need a mister,
Who would kiss a,
Girl like me.

Hello mister,
I'm Jacinta.
Would you kiss a,
Girl like me?

❧

I'm a little angel.
Short and stout.
Here is my halo.
Here is my pout.
When I become a devil,
I shout out.
Please be nice,
Or I'll be loud.

Try me, Baby. Throw a punch.
See if you can hit me.
Try me, Babe, because I have a hunch.
I bet that you will miss me.
Try me, Baby. Swing away.
Do you think that you can get me?
Try me, Babe, then run away.
Because the fear in you has met me.
Try me, Baby, if you're game.
You know that you can't beat me.
Try me, Babe, but you're insane.
This ends with you and me.

Simple
Muscles
In
Line
Everlasting

Lots
Of
Ventured
Emotion

The smile on your face.
The kisses in your text.
The sweet things you say.
And I anticipate what's next.

The surprise when you call.
You've got me on a tether.
Just one little tug.
And I know we'll be together.

There's a spark about you.
I see it with one look.
Everything about you.
Has got me hooked.

Can't stop thinking.
Can't stop liking.
Can't stop wanting you.
Can't stop thinking.
Can't stop loving.
Can't stop needing you.
Won't stop thinking.
Won't stop liking.
Won't stop wanting you.
Won't stop thinking.
Won't stop loving.
Until it's me and you.

❧

Falling for another man.
The boy who fills my fantasy.
Falling for another man.
The stud that's on the T.V.

Falling for another man.
Some other girl's reality.
He's a star. He plays guitar.
But he was never meant for me.

I want this sadness to be comforted by a friend.
For I know our laughter will be strong until the end.
I want all these tears to stop flowing from my face.
For I know all the good times will never be erased.
I want to find a way to mend a broken heart.
For a heart cannot live if it remains in two parts.
I want to know that there's a way for fear to fade away.
There's simply too much good in life to see the clouds remain.

❧

To my mother.
There'll never be another.
Who's quite as good as you.
And on this day,
I'd like to say.
That, Mummy, I love you.

❧

Power to the people.
Power to the girls.
Power to the ladies.
And women 'round the world.

REIMAGINED MOMENTS

❧❦

I'm so very happy, and this is clear to see.
But this is rather different, so very new to me.
I don't know why you make me laugh or how you make me smile.
But I'd like to take a moment and enjoy it for a while.
I'm holding on quite tightly, as this feeling is divine.
I don't want to see a day when this happiness isn't mine.

Every time I breathe, I feel you near me.
And every time I move, I think of you.
Reflect on what I have in life, and I know I don't have you.
Why must you play games with me?
Am I a toy to you?
The thought that comes so frequently,
Will you be my one, my true?
Maybe you can't hear my calls.
Or maybe you are blind.
Either way you break my heart,
With the way you play my mind.
Think about your actions.
And the imperfect things you say.
While you think that you are keeping me safe,
You're driving me away.

Don't say sorry.
It's too little too late.
Don't think I'll forgive you.
It's too little too late.
Don't pretend you care.
It's too little too late.
Don't expect me back.
It's too little too late.

Because you left me out in the cold.
Too many times.
You left me all alone.
Too many times.
You hurt me and I cried.
Too many times.
Said you loved me, but you lied.
Too many times.

Don't say that you were wrong.
Don't say that you stuffed up.
Don't say, "I'm sorry, please forgive me".
Because your time is up.
It's too little too late.
And you've done it way, too many times.

The world is full of beauties to make a person smile.
From the chirping birds to the buzzing bees.
Deserts and forests for miles.
There's something about your beauty that always makes me smile.
It could be your walk.
Or the way you talk.
Or perhaps it's your gentle smile.

Tiny toes and fingertips.
No bigger than a thumbtack.
Baby nose and eyelids.
Barely button size.
Little arms and legs for limbs.
A small and fragile head.
Watch her chest, as she takes a breath.
Each little fall and rise.

Strength can be our weakness.
Pain can fuel our health.
Friendship can make or break us.
And love can kill our trust.

Life can be contradictory.
It can be hard to understand.
Take our dear friend, Mickey Mouse,
Who'll never grow to be a man.

I'm sure you've loved him very much.
But do you see his side?
It's not his fault, poor Mickey,
As height has never been his pride.

Don't attempt to be much taller.
They won't see how hard you've tried.
And often times, when they say they care,
It turns out that they've lied.

Just be yourself from start to end.
There isn't a better way.
You're wasting your time if you try and pretend.
And the real you is better anyway.

REIMAGINED MOMENTS

❧

The clouds have left my head today.
There's nothing on my mind.
But I'm left with a swirling feeling.
Emotions intertwined.

When things are running smoothly,
It can only get worse from here.
I've got a nagging feeling,
That a breakdown is quite near.

I feel like I am losing it.
I've lost who I used to be.
I don't know who I am now.
I forgot how to be me.

I need someone to help me out.
I can't do this alone.
I need someone to love me.
To touch me close to home.

A breath of fresh air as I walk out the door.
A sigh of relief as I leave you.
A skip in my step as my feet hit the floor.
A smile because I know that I'm free of you.

I laugh as I joke with those I'll be leaving.
I cry for the friends I'll have lost.
I tie up loose ends and say my goodbyes.
And I smile at the thought I love most.

A breath of fresh air as I walk out the door.
A sigh of relief as I leave you.
Stay if you wish, but I won't anymore.
And I'll smile because I know that I'm free of you.

Draw the curtains. Close the door.
Remove distractions from the wall.

Turn off the light. Unplug the phone.
For the moment you're alone.

Shut your eyes. Block out the noise.
You're done with all those childish toys.

Go to sleep and hope you dream.
Things aren't always as bad as they seem.

When I was young and naïve,
Grownups told me not to lie.
But now that I am older,
I'm left wondering why.

People lie all around you.
Every second of the day.
I spent my life learning to tell the truth.
While others found another way.

This world can be a cruel place.
Difficult at best.
But aside the strife and struggle,
You'll find love amongst the rest.

Jumping with excitement.
Jump with joy, just jump with joy.
Jumping because you're hyped and,
Jump with joy, yeah jump with joy.
Jump, like there's no tomorrow.
Jump with joy, just jump with joy.
Jump like it doesn't matter.
Jump with joy, yeah jump with joy.
Jumping because you love it.
Jump with joy, just jump with joy.
Jumping like it's worth it.
And now jump with all your joy!

※

There's method to my madness.
And reason to my rhyme.
There's sense to why I say this.
Though I left sanity behind.

※

To my bro.
I hope you know,
The way I feel for you.
Little bro.
I hope you know,
That I'm so proud of you.

೭⊷ೋ

I am so very happy, so elated, don't you see.
Although this feeling is different, it's not so new to me.
You're no longer the one who makes me laugh, or the one who makes me smile.
I'm better on my own, you see. I've got self-confidence and style.
I don't live within your shadow now. I've come out of my shell.
I'm happier without you. So, you can go to hell.

Chills roll down my spine as the air grows colder.
The pain in my neck pinches, running across my shoulder.
I sigh a breath of longing. Where are you tonight?
I need you to hold me, warm and calm; everything alright.
I miss the world I used to know. I miss my friends and family.
I miss the sense that used to show. I miss the peace and serenity.

୬୶

A thumping head. Two eyes are sore.
A runny nose and my stomach wants more.
A run down me. A distant you.
While thoughts run wild, sane words run few.
Getting tired. Losing touch.
Wanting plenty. Not getting much.
Wish you were here to ease my pain.
To love my heart and keep me sane.

Such a beautiful night.
With the stars as our light.
Although the feeling's new.
I know that I want you.

With the moon in the sky.
And a twinkle in my eye.
I don't know how to move.
But I know that I want you.

It's been a long day.
And there's not much left to say.
No one here but us two.
And all I want is you.

I'm not sure where this going.
But anticipation has me glowing.
Today it felt like I flew.
Because all I want is you.

REIMAGINED MOMENTS

❧

Live your life to your fullest.
Let your fullest lead your life.
Make up all your own rules.
Face your fears and all your strife.

For every challenge that you come upon.
Tackle them with grace.
It's a big and scary world out there.
But you might just find your place.

Take each day, one at a time.
Wing it or make a plan.
Just be sure to tell them who you are.
And be clear on where you stand.

I wonder if this connection gets to you the way that it does me.
Sleepless after sleepless night, wondering what could be.
Though I resist, the struggle is real. It's been going on for a while.
But even though it bothers me, it always makes me smile.

I cannot eat, I cannot sleep, and I can hardly breathe.
I admit I think of you, but you don't make it easy.
You're keeping me awake, and you keep my body slim.
But the fact that I am breathless doesn't mean I'll let you in.

There's something here between us. But I'm not sure if it's good.
You think I'll cave eventually. But I'm not sure if I should.
I wish that this were easy; I wish that I could choose.
If by having you around, will I win, or will I lose?

REIMAGINED MOMENTS

༄

When you were sad, I dried your tears.
When you were scared, I eased your fears.
When you were weak, I carried you.
When you were angry, I was angry too.
When we were close together, nothing came between.
When we were apart, we were the dream team.
When we were at war, we were always friends.
When we were at peace, we could make amends.

But nothing's quite the same this time.
I feel the distance growing.
The tether snapped and I can't get it back.
Our golden light stopped glowing.
I have come to accept this reality.
The sad truth that seals our fate.
The friendship we once had is gone.
It will never be the same.

❧

You've been gone a while now.
I'm still alive.
So many went off with you.
I'm still alive.
And when I think about you and wish that I was with you.
I'm still alive.
But the truth is, my focus is misplaced, because while I am still alive,
In our hearts and our minds, it's you, not I, that's truly still alive.

As my heart is thumping madly, and my mind is spinning round.
I try to find a way to keep my feet firm on the ground.
You were always there for me. Even when you couldn't be.
You taught me how to be strong, brave, and true to me.
A mixed bag of emotions.
I'm sad, but I'll be ok.
Because I know deep within my heart.
We'll see you again one day.

Confusion running through my head.
I want to do the right thing.
I'm left with dos and don'ts instead.
And the trouble this will bring.

I don't know where to go from here.
Please grace me with some time.
I can't lose you because I love you, Dear.
But I need a little space that's mine.

A lot has changed. I've thought things through.
And now I know I don't need you.
Don't sook and whine and ask me "why?"
Just leave my sight. Just say goodbye.
Drop that attitude. You're not all that.
Just turn around, and don't come back!

Sitting here. It's very quiet.
Sitting here. There's not a sound.
Sitting here. I wish it wasn't.
Sitting here. I'm lost but found.
Sitting here. I think about you.
Sitting here. The way you are.
Sitting here. Wish you were with me.
Sitting here. Not close nor far.
Sitting here. There's not much to it.
Sitting here. I want you near.
Sitting here. There's nothing like it.
When you and I are sitting here.

൭൞

Love is the bloom of a rose.
The rose of sheer beauty.
The beauty of the soul.
The soul of life.
You are my life.
With you,
Love is.

Don't you just wish that the sky was purple,
And the grass was orange not green?
And don't you just wish that we could be together?
A love between you and me.
Don't you just wish that things were that simple?
Or that life was that easy?
Could you just imagine the life we would have,
If we had "you and me"?

❧

A sigh that's forceful – a sign that sleep is needed.
A sigh that's light – a breath of air exhaled.
A sigh that's drawn on – possibly a yawn.
A sigh with a smile – breathtaking happiness.

❧❦

I write poems that sound soft and sweet.
I play with words, making them match and meet.
But when it comes to writing poems for you,
I find myself wondering just what to do.

Should I write about your caring nature?
I take some time to think of you.
Or the way that you play roughly?
I just haven't got a clue.

It's just too hard to explain,
The person that you are.
Not enough words will ever come close.
You're an angel amongst the stars.

Something in the way you shine,
Brighter than the sun.
Draws us all toward you, Dear.
You're the epitome of fun.

ঞ٠ঞ

"Time flies when you're having fun."
"Time stopped still; I knew he was the one."
"It all slows down when life's a bore."
But do we really believe these sayings down to our core?

How can these sayings all fit together?
Time is something that goes on forever.
How does it stop? How can it start?
It doesn't have the rhythm of an ever-beating heart.

Time doesn't stop; it goes on until the end.
This is why you'll find, from time to time,
Fast or slow, if you're falling or on the climb,
It's all a waste without a friend.

✤

Breathing slowly, breathing calmly, each breath one by one.
You make me hyped and, so excited, make me want to run.
Taking time, to think about, what I am meant to do.
Going crazy, mind goes hazy, when I think of you.

Your touch so soft as I feel your fingers on my knee.
Your voice so smooth, melting the ice within me.
Your heart beats strong, making it hard for me not to show,
That I see your soul burn brightly. You're a beautiful man to know.

❧❦

You're so sexy. You're smooth and you're charming.
But bells are ringing in my head. I find them quite alarming.
Shh, I'll keep it hidden, so no one else will know.
My feelings buried deep within. On the surface, I won't show.

The tension here between us, I'll keep it to myself.
I wouldn't want to ruin it by telling someone else.
Can you even see it? Or is it just in my own mind?
A little brain teaser, and one that's not so kind.

❧

I am not religious, but I'm praying while I work.
For there's nothing I want more than for this to take.
You're already my whole world.
Even though you don't exist yet.
Because without you in my life,
I know my heart will surely break.

There are places I go in my head.
Lost in my mind, as I lie upon my bed.
Time all alone, in a place to call home.
There's no other place instead.

All alone in my little world.
No one but me, in my little world.
Silent and still, and nobody knows.
Silent and still, a soft little rose.

In the depth of a night like this.
In the thought of a mind like mine.
In the dream of a hearts' true wish.
In the place where there's no time.

Dream of a night like this.
With the thought of a mind like mine.
With the depth of a hearts' true wish.
Find a place where there's no time.

Such a place for a night like this.
Just a dream from a mind like mine.
It's the thought of a heart's true wish.
And the depth of "'til end of time."

❧

Trust is overrated. Yet underrated too.
Too many just don't understand. They haven't got a clue.
Do they understand it's meaning?
Do they really value it's worth?
Can you learn to truly trust another, during your time on earth?

Love is under-rated. This I wish you knew.
And if you open up your heart,
The toughest times, you will get through.
Many believe it a fantasy, but I can see it's true.
For I was one of the lucky ones, when I found love in you.

As I think of you, my heart pumps in my chest.
You've crept inside my mind, and my head won't let me rest.
I wish that I could find a way to ease my aching breast.
My obsession keeps on growing. You've become such a pest.

The way you walk. The way you talk.
Can't get you off my mind.
The way you move across the room.
And something snaps inside.
The way you glare. The way you stare,
With such sweet simple eyes.
The way your hand invites to stand,
So, we can dance all night.

As I think of you, my heart pumps in my chest.
Lying in my bed, I dream of how you are the best.

॰◦॰

I write about your eyes.
I write about your hair.
I write about your attitude.
How you don't seem to care.

But now it's time I stop,
And take a little drink.
It's time that I considered,
The way in which I think.

When I'm not around you,
I've a clear and conscious mind.
But then when I see you,
My thoughts get intertwined.

You make me go crazy.
Like never before.
You make me go crazy.
I'm desperate for more.

Only one thing can help me.
One thing to make me calm.
I know I won't be safe and sound.
Until I'm in your arms.

I'm crumpling at the edges.
The walls are caving in.
The boils are friends with blisters.
They're all across my skin.
I'm cracking under pressure.
The heat is killing me.
The flames tear at my flesh.
They burn from underneath.

❧

I see you in the sunlight.
I hear the poems that you write.
I cry.
I see you kiss her.
I see you near her.
I cry.
I hear your voice cry out.
I hear the words you shout.
I cry.
People insult you.
People compliment you.
I cry.
Then I ignore what people tell me,
As I'm told you love me.
And I cry.

❧❦

To my father,
Who brought me farther,
Than I could ever come.
With you around,
And the love we've found,
I feel that I have won.

❧❦

There's beauty in the world. You just have to see it.
There's beauty in yourself. You just have to be it.

There's beauty everywhere I look. I just have to believe it.
There's beauty deep within myself. I just have to free it.

༄༅

I am so very happy, so very full of glee.
And I'm enjoying this feeling. The feeling of being free.
I find the good in everything. I laugh and joke and smile.
There's so much more positive in my life. And there will be for a while.
There's no taking this away from me. Not a soul could do it.
The best I've felt in ages. And there isn't much else to it.

Sense and insanity.
To think you thought you knew me.
Until I told you what was going on,
Inside my silly mind.

Foolishness and sanity.
I shocked you with my mentality.
Leaving you stunned, psychologically,
Outside my silly mind.

Lost and confused.
You'll never understand me.
Just keep on trying, pathetically,
To find my silly mind.

The hardest part is accepting it.
You're never going to get to it.
You'll never understand it.
Life in my silly mind.

REIMAGINED MOMENTS

※

Words in a muddle.
Letters in a jumble.
Trying to make sense of the chaos in my mind.
Just put one word down.
Then another one beside it.
I keep ending up with the forward one behind.
Writing isn't hard; everybody does it daily.
Just one letter with another one beside.
Put them all together and you get a word, maybe.
Unless you're me. Then all you want to do is hide.

If clean can be messy.
And messy can be clean.
Then a bitch can be a dog.
And man-made, made by machine.

If people can be lost,
Even though they're clearly found.
Then maybe we are flying,
Even when we're on the ground.

The opposite of opposite,
Would make it just the same.
Why must the world be so convoluted?
Like a difficult, elaborate card game.

Who decides what's wrong and right?
Is it fate, or do we get a say?
When following rules can get you in trouble,
It's no wonder we struggle through each day.

Every day you see me.
Every day you smile at me.
You think that I don't see you.
But, Baby, you are wrong.

Every day I see you.
Every day I smile at you.
I know that you see me.
You know that I'm not wrong.

You know there's nothing stopping you.
Except your fears themselves.
Just look into a mirror.
You will only see yourself.

The one and only you.
That no one else can be.
The one and only you.
That's the one for me.

Don't you just wish that the sky was purple,
And the grass was orange not green?
And don't you just wish that the sun was red,
And that every night we had a blue moon?
Don't you just wish that the world would change,
And that everything would go your way?

Sometimes I wish that you didn't get sick.
And I think that you should have stayed.
And sometimes I wish that you didn't exist.
And then I wouldn't have to say,
That sometimes I wish that the world would change,
And that everything would go my way.

But...

Wishing doesn't change the past.
No matter what we've been through.
Wishing doesn't change a lot of things.
Like how much I miss you.

❦

Love isn't simple.
It's complicated.
Confusing.
Tiring.
Love at first sight isn't finding a hot guy.
It's connection.
Recognising souls.
Knowing.
Finding love isn't easy.
It's an adventure.
It's timing.
Looking for The One.
Keeping your love once you've got him?
Hard work.
Exhausting.
Heart breaking.
So, why bother?
Is love fun?
Is it really worth the work?
Only when you find true love, will you find out.

Fairy tales don't always come true.
But that's not the case when I'm with you.
You bring light to my world when I am down.
When I think I can't go on, you're always there to turn me around.
Through all the struggles you always make me smile.
Loving you has made my life worthwhile.

One poem after another. I'm angry and I'm sad.
I've crossed a river of emotions. There are few I haven't had.
But now I've found some happiness. I've worked out who to be.
It took some time, but I now know, simply how to be me.

You say you see me, but you never seem to hear me.
It's me against the world and I'm losing this war.
You say that you know me, but there's something you don't show me.
Some proof of understanding. Just a gesture, nothing more.

You treat me like a child. You try to keep me hidden.
Allowing me a chance to shine seems to be a chore.
Ease up and back off, it's not like I'm forbidden,
From seeing what's there, on the other side of the door.

I've had some time to think about, the way my life turned out.
When I try to do things right, it always ends with some self-doubt.
I didn't intend to end up this way. I just want to be me.
I don't know how else to explain myself. I just want to be free.

I'm sorry if you hate me, for something that I've done.
I want to keep you in my life, and fighting is no fun.
I hope you can forgive me. I hope that we can talk.
This world is big when you're on your own, and that's a path I don't want to walk.

When I'm reading. When I'm writing.
When I sit and watch TV.
When I'm talking. When I'm walking.
Wishing you were here with me.
When I'm resting. When I'm working.
When I take a breath to breathe.
When I'm sleeping. When I'm dreaming.
Dreaming you were here with me.
When I'm learning. When I'm teaching.
When I take some time to see.
When I'm thinking. When I'm knowing.
One day you'll be here with me.

Smile.
Every day is special.
Live today like it's your last.
Smile.
Don't let death dictate your life.
Or it'll come too fast.
Smile.
But don't deny your feelings.
Share them with those close.
Smile.
And remember the good times.
When they smiled the most.

JACINTA HUDSON

❧

Poems need rhymes.
But I haven't got the time.
You're giving all the signs.
But you're short a pickup line.

❧

Roses are red.
Violets are harsh.
I really like you.
So, don't be such an ass.

❧

You're doing my head in now.
My mind is spinning quite a bit.
No other way of putting it.
You're acting like a half-wit.

Would you please stop lying?
Be honest and stop denying.
Please just be yourself.
I don't want somebody else.

I want you to be mine.
You want "one-on-one" time.
There's another getting between us.
And I don't know who to trust.

Open up and talk to me.
I want you; don't you see?

❧❦

I know you like me, Baby.
Can't you tell me to my face?
I know you care about me.
Can't you tell me to my face?
I know your little secret.
Can't you tell me to my face?
I like you and I love you.
Now I've told you to your face.

❧

I loved you and you hurt me,
I don't miss you no more.
You dumped me and ignored me.
I don't miss you no more.
And now if you come near me,
I'll knock you to the floor.
I'll hurt you like you hurt me.
Because I don't miss you no more.

Are you who you want to be?
One thing I know is that I'm not me.
Just a stranger passing through.
Wishing I could be with you.
But I know I'm only wasting time.
Because I know deep down, you can't be mine.
So, I'll stick to the dreams I have while I sleep.
Just wishing with all my heart that you were mine to keep.
And I'll hope that I can find a way.
And that you'll call me your girl one day.

৯◌৵

Don't force me to feel.
I need time to heal.
And right now, I can't stand the aching.
Don't yell at me now.
When I don't know how,
To fight the wars I have been facing.
Don't come any closer,
As I need some closure,
Which I can't get with you standing over me.
Don't tell me what to do.
It's ok that I'm different from you,
And it's not fair that you underestimate me.

You held me in your arms, and I felt your warmth.
Close up against your chest I heard your heart.
You let me fall for you and then you left.
But I won't let this die or fall apart.

No, I'm going to hold my head up high,
And, as short as I am, stand tall.
Because as much as I don't know what I want,
I know "friends" won't do at all.
I'm going to have you in my arms,
The same way we did that day.
Or at least that's what I'm hoping for,
If I can get my way.

ঞ্জ

With stars in the sky, and a sparkle in your eye.
There's nowhere I'd rather be.
Under candlelight, in the dark of night.
There's nowhere I'd rather be.
With a home cooked meal, and the warmth I feel.
There's nowhere I'd rather be.
Your arms wrapped around me. Your kisses lightly on my cheek.
There's nowhere I'd rather be.
I don't want to go tonight; I just want to hold you tight.
And never let you leave me.
For I can't seem to let you go. There's something that you need to know.
There's nowhere I'd rather be.

❧

I want the past to be a dream.
It made me who I am it seems.
But you know it's killing me.
And I don't know just who to be.

❧

Wanting clarity of mind.
But some things are hard to find.
Trying to work out what I need.
Needing to be freed.
I'm a blimp of life in time.
But the blip of life's not mine.
Are you who you want to be?
For I know that I'm not me.

☙❧

Short and simple things are good,
To make another smile.
So, let's have a cuppa and a laugh.
Pop your feet up and stay a while.

☙❧

Just one little kiss for those that I miss.
A hug for those I wish were here.
A cuddle in bed for those stuck in my head.
And all my heart for those I've loved all year.

❧

A bundle of joy for the whole world to see.
Not a toy but a baby.
Soft as a dove, and you'll never love.
Another thing quite like this baby.

❧

A love so close to the heart, will never go away.
A love that will never part, will surely always stay.

※

I'm sitting here and thinking all the things that crowd my mind.
And the more I think about these things, the more I feel behind.
Chaotic thoughts are getting to me, and I don't have a hold,
On how I am to figure them out. They're problems left unsolved.

Those around me add to the mess, telling me what to believe.
They don't know that I've got tricks, stored safely up my sleeve.
Maybe they are right. Maybe I will fail.
But it's my mind, and it's my life, and on these I won't bail.

❦

My peace and serenity, as a gale force wind blows outside.
Leaves on trees have no hope. Roots buckle down, ready for the ride.

The windows rattle and the doors all creek.
Pillows over tired heads as people try to sleep.

Despite the noise of the storm around, I feel so calm inside.
I'm safe in here, not scared at all; I feel no need to hide.

I close my eyes and listen in; how long will this storm go.
I wonder if a breeze will remain in the morning, or if the sun will show.

❧

I want to say I'm happy, and I want to say congrats.
But I'm curious and cautious because I've met so many rats.
I can see that she is happy. It makes me jealous in a way.
You love each other oh so much; you'd marry in a day.
So, I'll jump abord this loving train. I'll hide away my glare.
I'll bury all my cynicism and embrace this loving pair.
I'm going to say I'm happy, and I'm going to say congrats.
Because, although I'm cautious, I know you're not one of those rats.

❧

Confusion running through my mind. I don't know what to do.
When the rest of my life is sorted out, it all comes back to you.
Mixed between emotions. I feel trapped but also free.
Only knowing that I want you, and hoping you want me.

I've weighed up all the pros and cons, the gloomy and the glad.
Although I know there's good things there, I focus on the bad.
I wish you'd help me fix this mess; I want to make you see.
That all I want is to be your girl; I'm hoping you want me.

JACINTA HUDSON

※

I think I really like you.
What I don't understand,
Is if you like me too,
Why won't you be my man?

Of me are you ashamed?
Is my childishness to be blamed?
Did I do something wrong?
Did I sing an annoying song?

Do you think I'm just a flirt?
Is it down to the length of my skirt?
Is there something about who I am?
I just don't understand.

I don't know what it is about you.
I find you so beguiling.
I just don't want to feel blue.
And you always keep me smiling.

REIMAGINED MOMENTS

Every time I breathe, I feel you near me.
And every time I move, I think of you.
And when somebody says your name,
I stare into space, and I feel all the shame.

As days go on, as times pass by,
I get over you, but I still ask why.
Why you treated me like that.
Why every day you lied.
What did I do?
What have I done?
You walked away, you left me there.
We went from two to none.

You're over me, I see that now,
But though I try, I can't see how.
How you could treat me like that.
How you treat me now.

Every day as you walk by,
You ignore me, as I sigh.
I've worked out now, that you don't care.
And yes, I think that it's not fair.

Before I go, I have to say,
That every week and every day,
I sit and cry, I sit and laugh,
And deep inside I know I trust,
The fact that I still love you.

❧

I know you want me.
I know you need me.
There's no big secret.
I want you too.

I know you love me.
I know you, Baby.
There's no big secret.
I love you too.

When I look into your eyes, you know I see it.
And then when I look into your smile, you know I feel it.
Baby there is nothing you can hide. Come on, believe it.
Then, Baby, look into the crystal sky, you know you need it.

Walk before you run.
Sit before you stand.
I need you here now, Hun.
So, come on be my man.

Your breath, your mouth, the way you touch.
Your eyes, your hair I love so much.
Your smile, your style, your humour too.
Your strength of character no one breaks through.

Your grin, your glare, your silly smirk.
Your carefree attitude adds a stress-free quirk.
Your care, your love, your protective side.
Your skill to see through what I can't hide.

Your willingness to stop the world, if ever I did ask.
Your ability to see through me, beyond my careful mask.
Your sense and sensibility, your nature, and your spirit.
Your honesty, your loyalty, you stand by me right through it.

Your arms when wrapped around me tight.
Your soothing words that make it right.
Your thoroughness in everything you do.
Your golden touch that makes me need you.

Get out, get out, get out.
You're clouding up my thought space.
Get out, get out, get out.
You're crowding up my mind.
Get out, get out, get out.
You're clouding up my heart space.
Get out, get out, get out.
You're crowding all the time.
Get out, get out, get out.
Distractions and confusions,
Get out, get out, get out.
Have me spinning 'til I'm blind.
Get out, get out, get out.
I need a little space inside.
Get out, get out, get out.
Some space inside that's mine.

We're all going to miss you.
Because you were always there.
We're all going to miss you.
Right now, it doesn't seem fair.
We're all going to miss you.
Because you've gone away.
We're all going to miss you.
It's hard to smile today.
We're all going to miss you.
We all wished you could've stayed.
We're all going to miss you.
But we'll meet again one day.

Take it slow.
Just let go.
Surrender and release.
Because you know,
If you just breathe,
He's simply there to please.

Open your heart.
And close your eyes.
Then throw your arms out wide.
Breathe in his kiss,
As you kiss his lips.
Then let him come inside.

Stop. Breathe.
Take a step back.
Stop. Breathe.
Take a moment to react.

Stop. Breathe.
Before you fall apart.
Stop. Breathe.
And listen to your heart.

꙳

I'm telling you I don't eat much, but you won't stop and listen.
What part of my life story do you really want to hear?
I'm trying to help you understand, but I can't see the point.
What reason will be enough for you, for my voice to ring out clear?

I'm a very small girl, from a rather small family,
And we only eat small meals. Does that help you sleep at night?
I'm a very picky eater, from a family of picky eaters.
I don't stand out amongst them. Is that going to be alright?

Look, I have a funny tum – suppose I got it from my mum.
I guess it could be worse though, and I don't have that fight.
Some people have a chronic illness – but mine is not as bad as this.
She taught me to get past it. Does this help you see the light?

Let's talk about my sister. Despite her need for fatty food,
At six was anorexic. Does that help you understand?
Is there something you want me to say, to help you get along your way?
Can I be done with this now, or is there more that you demand?

How about my model grandmother, who was stunning to the end?
Some say I look just like her. She had really gentle hands.
Try to remember that I'm not a child. I can make my own decisions.
That I'm happy and I'm healthy, just exactly as I am.

❧

Happiness bundled up in sweet balls of candy.
Denial in the shape of lollies, making me feel younger.
Smiles on daises, daffodils, and dandelions.
Laughter coming from far away, probably the cave of wonders.

Insanity gets a hold of me,
The way sanity holds on to you.
You think I'm broken and scattered around.
But you can put me back together with some glue.

Take a look into the looking glass,
But watch your head on the crystal ball.
The cards will appear, but nothing will seem clear.
It's too late by then, as your underneath my thrall.

Don't try to work it out; you'll give yourself a headache.
You're hoping I'll make sense, but you can't see me through your lens.
You think you'll beat me in this race, but you're already far behind.
You'll worry for my mental health. But it's *you* that's lost your mind.

Music blasting in my ears, I fight to ignore the world.
Eyes are fighting back the tears, they fall anyway, like diamonds or pearls.
My heart beats in my chest, loud and strong and proud.
The music changes and I choke, my thoughts and feelings clashing, like thunder from a cloud.

I try to breathe myself through the pain, it just moves, from my heart to my gut.
I'm in such a mess now, an intense emotional rut.
I keep coming back to this place, I never see it coming.
And it hurts just the same every time, drumming, humming, numbing.

I know I have the strength to move on, but I can't seem to find it.
I search for something to pick me up, but it all backfires, every little bit.
Lost in confusion, anger, and despair, directed at many things and nothing.
Feeling everything and nothing, and I want affection, just anything, something.

Someone to hold me and tell me it's alright, even if they need to lie.
Cheer me up for now, fix the problem later, or at least try.
Kiss me goodnight and leave it at that.
We'll deal with the rest tomorrow, but for now I just want small chat.

❧

It's so very loud in here, although there's not a sound.
The music playing, the windows banging, I'm lost but I am found.

So many voices in my head, it's twelve and I can't sleep.
I wish that I were in a land, of dreaming, oh so deep.

Specifics I can't tell you, as I don't even know.
Of feelings on the surface, and those that I can't show.

In my head, I wish there were, a way to understand.
The things I think are such a mess, and now I need a hand.

I need to sort through all these thoughts but haven't got the time.
Half an hour later, and I am still in rhyme.

I know that I can work it out, of this I promise you.
I know that I can work it out, I'm just not sure on how to.

Don't pick up the phone.
Don't answer the door.
Don't dare to reply to my texts.
Don't smile to my face.
Don't look my way.
Don't wait for what comes next.

Don't keep up with old friends, to see how I am.
Don't ask about me at all.
Don't question my reasons or reason my motives.
Don't ever answer my calls.

Don't expect apologies.
Don't wait for forgiveness.
Don't assume that I'll show up at your door.

Don't wait for "hello" or "goodbye" when we pass.
Don't think I'll send a birthday card as the time will pass.

Don't ask me why.
Don't think I'll explain.
Don't think that you're above it all, or that you're not to blame.

Don't wait until it blows over.
Don't think I'll hold a grudge.
Don't think that you know me, because it's clear that you don't.
Don't pretend you care, because in the end you won't.

❧

My head is spinning.
Feel like I'm sinking.
Falling further down.
My blood is pumping.
Heart keeps thumping.
Getting really loud.
Mind is churning.
Thoughts keep turning.
I'm lost but I am found.
Emotions rising.
Getting hyped and,
Spinning round and round.

❧

I can tell that I am bored.
Because I'm writing a lot today.
But the problem is that I'm so bored.
I haven't that much to say.

The inspiration you gave me.
The motivation that saved me.
Forever and always, you are there for me.
And I will love you until the end of time.

REIMAGINED MOMENTS

JACINTA HUDSON

BONUS POEMS
(Adults Only)

NOTE FROM THE AUTHOR

The following is a selection of poems I wrote toward the end of drafting Just a Thought. I decided not to include them back then because my pitch was often "poems written though my teen years" and these were not.

Not only were these poems written after my teen years, but they had a much more adult vibe to them. Some angry, many sexual, they didn't fit the overall vibe of Just a Thought.
So, when I was selecting the 100 poems I would publish (out of approximately 125 drafted) it made sense to leave these ones out for the sake of continuity.

Please keep in mind that if you're sharing this book with teens, the following poems may not be appropriate for younger readers.

಄

I've played this game before.
Do this. Do that. You're always right and I'm always wrong.
You treat me like shit, and then throw me to the floor.

But you don't know I've played this game before.
You'll continue your charade. Throw a fit every time.
That's ok, you don't know, that I've put up with more.

Because I've played this game before.
You keep pushing me to the edge, but everyone has their limit.
I wonder if you'll see it coming before I walk out the door.

You'll soon see, I've done it before.

Shut your face. You don't know what you're talking about.
Shut your mouth. You don't know who I am.
You shut your mind; because of course you're always right.
Then you shut your eyes, because you decided that you can.
You're shutting everyone around you out. Including those who care.
So, shut your face. Just shut your mouth.
Because I'm sick of this shit. It just isn't fair.

REIMAGINED MOMENTS

༄༅

Romancing me is not easy.
Unless my beau is you.
Because you know I'm not flimsy.
Unless I'm fucking you.

༄༅

You're hard and I'm soft.
You're a man and I am not.
You know all the moves to make me lose the plot.
And when you touch me there, you really hit the spot.

I run my fingers through my hair.
You're trapped inside my mind.
Every nerve in my body on edge.
I want you all the time.

Tingling touches across my skin.
I think of how you held me so.
But if I break down and let you in.
I'll never want to let you go.

I brace myself for the best and the worst.
And I'm always left surprised.
I want to seize the day and get a little carried away.
I just want to let you inside.

His breath smells sweet as you breathe him in.
His touch is soft and warm.
His strokes on your skin light a fire within.
And you know that he's ready to perform.

His kiss is hot and wet on you.
Sending tingles down your spine.
Then he whispers softly in your ear,
"I want you to be mine."

❧❦

Sitting here, in this heat, sweat running down my body.
Sitting here, I think of you, rubbing ice over my body.
Lying here, in this heat, I think about your body.
Lying here, I think of you, up against my body.
Wish you were here, in this heat. Bring with you your body,
Then we could move and make the heat. You up against my body.

How I'd love to rip your shirt off.
And kiss those supple lips.
How I'd love to take those pants off you.
And sway close to your hips.

How I'd love so much to be with you,
And hold you close to me.
You'll make me wet. You'll make me sweat.
Please make me beg and plea.

Much more than hugs and kisses.
Feel the heat from top to toe.
Turn me on, the way you can.
Proving *you* love *me* the most.

I want to run my hands across your shoulders.
I want to take them downward. Should I dare?
I want to lay kisses along your jaw line.
I want your mouth to touch me everywhere.

I want to reach for places I can't see.
I want you to search for places deep inside of me.
I want to feel the heat as our bodies dance.
As we slam into the passion that we share.

REIMAGINED MOMENTS

※

Lay me on the table.
Or prop me up onto a chair.
Keep my feet firm on the ground.
Or lift me high into the air.

Come and touch me baby.
Make me feel like I'm the one.
Come and kiss me deeply.
Let's get down and have some fun.

Don't go over thinking it.
Just come and touch my skin.
My heart and body are here for you.
And I want to let you in.

JACINTA HUDSON

⁂

The feel of his gaze on her skin.
The heat of fire from within.
The touch of his fingers across her face.
In the way that he does with such grace.

The roll of his tongue in each kiss.
They're bodies so close they can't miss.
The rub of their thighs become tight.
Then both cry out with all their might.

ಹೇಗೆ

You say that you care.
But you don't give a fuck.
I hope you get hit by a truck.

ಹೇಗೆ

Arrogant, self-centred, patronising prick!
I hope you get a boner and then someone snaps your...

INTERVIEW WITH THE AUTHOR

with Alex Clifford

INTERVIEW WITH THE AUTHOR

ALEX:
Just a Thought is ten years old and while so many things about ourselves and the world around us has changed, your dedication to writing poetry has not. What motivates your creativity?

JACINTA:
Poetry is easy for me. In the sense that love and emotion are in my core and that's what drives me. Poetry has come from that place. It's just been like breathing. It's just that thing that I just *do*.

For a long time, that worked against me. I didn't call myself a poet, I just wrote some poems. It was so natural that it was a shrug-it-off thing.
I also find that I'm so used to it coming easy – when I allow it to – that when I don't make time to reflect on my emotions, I end up ignoring that part of me completely, and I end up not writing anything. So, it works against me in that sense too – I end up taking it for granted at times.

But in the same sense, going forward, I want to make it work *for* me. By *forcing* myself to sit down and let it come "easy" – which I realise is an oxymoron. [laughs] I want to utilize the ease to build something [poetry collection] to support the foundation of something that isn't easy. [i.e., novel writing]

ALEX:
As someone who's so overwhelmed with stuff, what do you do in terms of finding the time to write?
When you very first started writing poetry, what were you doing?

JACINTA:
[I was doing] Nothing. That was the beauty of it.
If you go back to the very start [writing poems in high school], I would be writing them in class and in my private study sessions. I just needed a break from life. It wasn't about writing poems, it was about getting my thoughts and feelings out so I could breathe and think clearly.
Sure, some poems from *Just a Thought* were written after graduating high school, but a LOT of my initial poetry was written in a classroom or in a private study session – or even on the bus ride to or from school. My school planners were littered with poems. And at the end of the year, if I hadn't already, I would go through and take all the poems out and put them in a notebook, or in a word document, together. And that's how *Just a Thought* got started in the first place. Just random poems thrown together.

NOW is a very different story.
Now, I'm *forcing* myself to find time to *allow* myself to reflect on stuff to put in a poem. It's a very weird sensation to me. I've come to realise that the time and mental space I had back then was something I really took for granted.
Now, because I have so much going on, I have a lot of mental strain and overwhelm. So, I don't have the same writing process.
Actually, a good chunk of the poems I've come up with in the last couple of years have been in the shower, because it's the only time I

let myself *think*. Much like when you're standing in the shower and you relax your muscles, I actually relax my mind and let it wonder. I'm not distracted by thoughts of making phone calls or social media posting, because I can't do that stuff in the shower anyway. So, that stuff doesn't clog up my mind. I have a very mini holiday to let my mind wander, reflect on how I feel, and play with words without the pressure to get it right. But outside of that, I need to actively stop and say, "I need to write some poems. If I'm going to publish more poetry books, I need to *make time* to write poems."

ALEX:
Would you consider yourself more of an authentic writer? Rather than a purpose driven writer?

JACINTA:
100%. I can't stand categories, I can't stand genres, I can't stand this concept that things have to happen in a certain way.
Let me clarify. I understand the purpose and benefits of having specific genres and categories, don't get me wrong. My issue lies in the concept that a writer should stick to a certain genre or category. To think in that space, write in that space, publish and market in that space… And to never veer from that.
It's something I've never vibbed with as a reader or an author. While I do often gravitate to similar books, I actually don't like reading the same genre book after book. I need variety in my reading, or I get bored. And the same goes for my writing. Yes, I've started with a heavy poetry presence, and many of my novel ideas are YA contemporary, but some of my favourite book ideas are actually Adult contemporary, Adult Historical, and a YA with magical realism.
My point is that I will always write from where the heart of my stories are, which will mean a lot of variety – which I think is pretty special.

ALEX:

Do you think that played a role in you starting your author career with poetry rather than a book? Aside from not being ready to tell the story that you wanted to tell, but because you do enjoy bits and pieces?

JACINTA:

Maybe. I was always writing stories alongside poems, but it was snippets of stories and random scenes [vignettes]. I guess the poetry came first because I had more of it. I had enough poems to put into a book, but I didn't have enough of a story to publish a novel.
And maybe there is some "bits and pieces" in the poetry. The variety of my emotions (and the poems that came from them) made it easy to create enough content for a book because I wasn't bogged down in one plot with one character – rather it was 100 different characters with 100 different stories to tell through emotion.

ALEX:

Considering your dislike of structure/genre, what's your plan going forward in regard to self-publishing or traditional publishing? And why?

JACINTA:

I'll always continue to self-publish my poetry. I want it done my way, and I want it done in my time. And that's something only I can control. What's more, if a publishing house ever said they wanted to publish my poetry, I don't believe they'd do it with the heart I would put in on my own.

But I would rather see my novels traditionally published. I don't know why.
In this weird and unexplainable way, I don't think that I can do a *novel* justice on my own. Sure, I can do what I'm qualified for and

outsource help for the rest and self-publish, but I don't feel confident that I'd do it right. Ask me again in 10 years and that might change, I don't know.

Traditional publishing scares the crap out of me actually. Because I'm not a patient person, so the idea of querying and being in the trenches and being on submission and all that terrifies me. But the flip side of that is, I don't like to do things in a rush and I'm not very good with deadlines and if you tell me to do something I shut down. So, who knows if I'm even cut out for the traditional route? All I know is that I have an idea of the path I want to take, and I'll work out the rest later. First, I have to finish- and edit, and edit, and edit- a novel to publish. [laughs]

ALEX:
Considering everything comes back to emotion – that's your thing… Can you tell me about your personal emotional experience of releasing *Just a Thought* the first time, and how does it compare to releasing the new-and-improved version, *Reimagined Moments*, this time?

JACINTA:
That's a good question!
The crazy thing is, it's completely backwards to what people would expect…

Where most people are super nervous to publish their debut book, I was so casual and flippant about wanting to "try" publishing. I did very little research into how to publish and decided self-publishing in some form was going to be the way to go.
When I published with Xlibris in 2012, I just threw everything together and handed it over with a "you guys know what you're doing so you'll be able to fix it up" attitude. My logic was very

carefree, figuring, if people buy it then cool, if they don't then whatever. It was very carefree and spontaneous.

And now…
It *means* something now. I *care* now.
I've rewritten these poems so that they don't make me cringe anymore. I had some poems where what I was writing was so lame, but I couldn't think of any words that would rhyme and make sense, so I'd just throw in anything that I could think of. I was so set on having the emotion and the reflection of the moment be completely true to that moment that I would refuse to change the wording. If it sounded wrong, it was deliberate- because that was the emotion of that moment. Sometimes emotions don't make sense.
But looking back and rewriting them, I groan. I could have rewritten a word, or a line here and there, and still have the same emotion come through.

So now, I care. I've reworked most of the poems and I've put them into a different order to have flow a better flow now. I spend a lot of time on the order of my poems these days, ensuring the reader has a good ebb and flow of poems, and that "random" isn't jarring.

And that's the biggest difference between then and now across the board. I'm putting the effort- in writing, formatting, cover etc.- into doing it RIGHT.

ALEX:
Do you think it took you 10 years to get to that point? Or was it more of a strategic move, to wait for 10 years?

JACINTA:
No! No way. I've had this in motion for a while.

For many years now I haven't really loved *Just a Thought* and wondered if I would ever rerelease it. I realised I was going to do it when I was working on *Emotional Ramblings*.

I came up with this idea that I was going to make a brand-new collection of poetry. I was going to do a whole collection with matching covers, make the flow of the poems more fluid, and publish a new book once every 1-2 years.

When I saw that 10-year anniversary for *Just a Thought* would be coming up this year, that's when I very deliberately planned to have *Emotional Ramblings* AND *When Straight Lines Aren't* published before this book. And I was insistent on doing both- despite having a baby and the pandemic and some of the struggles I had getting those books out- because I didn't want to call it a "new" collection, but just rerelease *Just a Thought*. I was making a point of showing people I was serious about an entirely new collection first.

When Straight Lines Aren't (ironically) made me jump a lot of hurdles and I wanted to give up on so many times. I would be stressed out of my mind and people asking me if I really wanted to publish, and I would say "I HAVE to." I didn't care if it only had 50 poems in it, I was getting it out there. I was making a point that these will all sit on your shelves one day together as a *collection*.

ALEX:

As I understand it, your formatting choices are quite deliberate. Tell me more about why you format your books the way you do – without titles, all mixed together and without structure?

JACINTA:

Put simply, I don't title or number my poems because I believe in them standing on their own emotional foundation.

For me, in my experience, I find that if you group, title or number poems it gives the reader a predisposed inclination of what the author suggests they *should* feel about it – before ever reading a line.

I format my poems in a deliberate attempt to eliminate that predisposition.

I figure that if you've read a poem of mine and not understood the *emotion*, I haven't written it properly. You should not need a cue to know what emotion is being portrayed – or at least to form your own interpretation of what emotions may be being expressed. You should be like, "Yep, that is an angry poem." "That bitch was sad when she wrote that." "Ok, now I want a baby, because that was emotional." I want that emotion to stand on its own and tell the story without the need of a prompt. You shouldn't have to know what the poem is about or even understand the story behind it, to feel the emotion being portrayed- and that's what I'm going for.

I know some people like the idea of titles or groups to help guide the reader, and some readers like to get a sense of what is coming before they start reading. But for me it is distracting. I don't like being told how to feel about a poem before I read it.
And there have been many times I have written something about one topic and a reader has expressed that they resonated with it because of a completely different scenario. They have made their own assumption about where the emotion has come from, and what the poem is about, based on their own experience, and thereby given it a new life in the new interpretation. I love that by not suggesting it's meaning in a grouping or title, I open each and every poem up to be more than what it is in my own mind.

ALEX:
What would you say to yourself of 10 years ago? To the version of yourself that was just about to publish *Just a Thought* in all the state you were in, what would you say?

JACINTA:
Keep writing.
I don't believe in changing the past – so advising my past self to do more research, promote more, work harder etc would be completely pointless. But I do believe in learning from every experience. I had been convinced that you wouldn't make a career out of creative passions, and so I practically put the pen down altogether after *Just a Thought*.
But, in my experience, putting the pen down after *Just a Thought* was so detrimental to my career. Sure, to some degree, walking away meant that when I came back to it, I came back with a fire that was hard to ignore, shoving me toward writing like it was my destiny. But it was so hard to get back into that headspace after so long away from it.
So, keep writing. Don't put the pen down and walk away. You don't have to do anything with it, you don't have to publish or anything, just keep writing. Don't lose the passion just because you don't think you'll make a career out of it.

ALEX:
Since you wrote so much of *Just a Thought* in high school, if a year 12 student picked up your book, what would be the message you would want them to get from your work or from you? What would you say to people who feel the kind of depression and anxiety that you experienced in your youth?

JACINTA:
Don't be *afraid* of your emotions.
People are very quick to withdraw from what they're feeling, hide from it or mask it. Whether you express it outwardly or whether you just sit in it, whether you write or do something else creative with it, whether you just vent it and let it out to a friend… Whatever it is, don't be *afraid* of it.

Emotions of all kinds are with us all the time. And it breaks my heart to see full grown adults who don't want to acknowledge the emotions they have- from the fear of judgement if they show sadness, to the hesitation to accept good news on the off chance it's a prank.
Acknowledging it doesn't make it any better or worse, it just makes it there.

And that's what I think people get out of my books- it's there. It's sitting in the back of their minds and they're ignoring it, and then they're read my words and they go "oh, that's what I've been feeling." But it was always there. I just brought it out of you because I was aware enough to pull it out of me.

Very much like when people say, "just BE you." I say, "just FEEL you." Be ok with feeling how you feel.

Being afraid of being sad won't change if you're depressed or not. Being afraid of being happy won't change if things are going well in your life or not. It's just the emotion. And it blows my mind that there are people out there that don't want to really *feel* the way they feel. You don't have to express it outwardly if you don't want to. But it's important to feel the way you genuinely feel.
Because it's literally like holding in a fart. It's not going to help you to hold it in. It will still be there, bottling up. And it's probably going to do you more damage that way. You don't have to let it out, but you're not going to be able to NOT feel it if you hold it in. Because it's only going to swell.

ALEX:
Do you have a favourite poem from *Just a Thought/Reimagined Moments*? Do you have a favourite poem from any of your books?

JACINTA:

Yes! My all-time favourite poem hasn't changed in the entire time I've been writing. Some have come close, and many have very emotional places in my heart, that will never change. But there has always been something very special about this poem that has made it stand out from the rest.

I think it's because so much of my poetry drafting is such an emotional experience, but this one was a little more mental – more like word play than emotional expression.

I think another reason is how it came about. I wrote this one when waking up one morning. It had no logical or emotional catalyst – it just *was*. I woke up, reached over for a notebook, and began writing. I think it came from my soul rather than my heart *or* my mind. It just seemed to demand to be written. Like it had a life of its own, long before my pen hit the page.

In the depth of a night like this.
In the thought of a mind like mine.
In the dream of a hearts' true wish.
In the place where there's no time.

Dream of a night like this.
With the thought of a mind like mine.
With the depth of a hearts' true wish.
Find a place where there's no time.

Such a place for a night like this.
Just a dream from a mind like mine.
It's the thought of a heart's true wish.
And the depth of "'til end of time."

ALEX:
Besides your poetry, what else are you up to?

JACINTA:
Oh goodness! What a loaded question.
The best part about this question will undoubtedly be looking back at this book in another ten years and reflecting on everything I have done in that time, so thank you for asking.
Let's see. As I write this, I am working on…
- Rewrites for my Historical Love Story: My grandmothers life story, following her relationship with love throughout the years. We follow her from early childhood right to the end, seeing love, in all its forms, through her eyes.
- Expanding my range of Downloadable Templates
- Taking submissions for my Parenting Poems Collaboration.
- Half outlining/half drafting my Adult Contemporary trilogy
- Drafting for my new poetry book (and planning between 7-10 more in the next 10 years)
- Being a mum and a partner to my two favourite boys
- Brainstorming some ideas for future merch options…
… and a few other things I have up my sleeve.

ALEX:
What can we expect from you in the future?

JACINTA:
A lot.
A lot of books, a lot of emotion, a lot of jumping around trying new things.
I want to fill readers shelves with my poetry books and novels.
I want to fill minds with thoughts of, "I didn't think about it like that."
I want to fill hearts with love and compassion and understanding.

And I'll do all that by putting my heart into my work, and always trying to do things a little differently than everyone else.

Honestly, my goal is just to keep doing what fuels my passion for writing, in whatever direction that takes me. If that means I let go of a bunch of stuff in the next year and focus on poetry, that's ok. If it means poetry gets left behind to make way for bigger and better things, I will roll with that.

All I know is that I won't limit myself by expectations or popular themes. I plan to do *what I want*, according to my own timeline, even if that seems chaotic and senseless to others. Because somewhere along the line I'm sure people will start to understand what I'm like, how I think, and all that, and embrace the emotional chaos behind each new step. [laughs] I want my career as an author to always seem authentic to who I am and the stories, and emotions, I have to share.

ALEX:
Is there anything else you'd like your readers to know about your books or your writing journey?

JACINTA:
I want my poetry books to grow. Both as a collection and individually.
I want to have more poems in each book, and for each book to take up more space on a shelf next to the rest of the collection.
I want my books to be impactful.

I love the idea of my books giving people that "woah" moment.
"Woah, that emotion really got me."
"Woah, I did not see that coming."
"Woah, that cover really stands out."
"Woah, what a cool collection sitting on that shelf."

"Woah, I did not see poetry being this modern or this cool or this easy to relate to." I want my books to stand out on the shelf, in stores, and in readers hearts and minds.

THEN & NOW

*Behind the Scenes of
Just a Thought – Reimagined
Moments*

A lot has changed since I first published *Just a Thought*, so I thought it would be fun to take a look back on where this journey started and where I am now.

Here's a look at the then and now comparisons, along with some fun facts about *Just a Thought / Reimagined Moments*.

	Just a Thought	Reimagined Moments
# Original Poems:	100	42- Poems with less than 2–3-word changes are considered "original". Less than 5 are exactly as they were in *Just a Thought*.
# Rewritten Poems:	0	58- from 4+ word changes, some with major overhauls.
# Bonus Poems:	0	8 in the main pages. 13 in bonus poems section in back of the book.
Time it took to write/edit:	Approx. 10 years.	Approx. 2 months.

When it was written:	2002- 2012	2021
When it was published:	2012	2022
My age when publishing:	22	32
How many poems I had written when publishing:	100 published + 21 unpublished	408 original 58 rewritten 21 bonus Approx. 155 drafted for next book
Published with:	Xlibris	KDP/Ingram Spark
Cost to publish: (Including editing, formatting, cover, marketing materials etc)	Approx. $700 (Exact figures lost to time)	Approx. $263 for cover design Approx. $64 to upload to Ingram Spark

Fun Facts, Part 1: The Poems.

Page 9: Written about my sister. If you go back and compare the original to the rewrite, you can actually see my growth from a young girl in pain to a woman who has healed to some degree.

Page 58: This was actually written about a paper plate, burning in a bonfire.

Pages 11, 13, 50, 51, 98 & 99: These were all removed from the original draft. They didn't fit as smoothly as others, so I kept them in a document titled "bonus poems" in case I ever wanted to do an anniversary edition- and now you get to read them too!

Pages 19, 31 & 61: Written as a set. I deliberately split them up because I didn't want to sound repetitive. These (and other poems, where you see similar lines repeated) are a sign of days when I couldn't get my thoughts and emotions out in *one* poem, so I kept trying until I got it right. This repetition also happened where I came back to a poem because it was about the same person or situation and imitated the vibe/rhythm to express the emotion as a situation has evolved.

Page 24: This was my favourite poem for a very long time because I resonated with the message so much. By the time I had published it, I didn't like it anymore because my writing voice had changed so much since penning and it sounded a bit corny to me. Being able to rewrite it and give it new life made me so happy, and while it still has a touch of corniness, I am much more happy with the vibe of the new version.

Page 30: This poem was originally the last poem of the book, as I thought it summed up the chaotic nature of *Just a Thought*- and my emotional rollercoaster over the prior 10 years. I moved it because it no longer felt like a final thought. My poetry makes more sense to me now. My books no longer feel chaotic and thrown together, but more natural, an extension of myself.

Page 53: My all-time favourite poem! It is my equivalent of having a dream and turning it into a novel. I woke up one morning with words floating in my head, so I grabbed the nearest notepad. I had no idea what I was writing- the emotion or the message- but just started. After putting the first stanza down it felt unfinished, and in an attempt to write a second stanza, I found myself using the same words in a different order. When I noticed that it somehow still made sense, I tried for a third, as a sort of creative brain game. When *that* worked, I decided it was complete and left it as is. My favourite thing about this poem is when people tell me it doesn't make any sense, and then they reread it and change their minds. I love its vibe, the flow of the words, and that understanding it is a bit of a poetic brain twister.

Page 60: Originally, this poem was half the size. Another example of a poem that has grown with me, expanding to reflect my own growth.

Page 64: Another favourite that was ruined by a corny ending. Rewrites have taken the cringe out of this poem, making it feel less forced.

Page 79: Inspired by Britney Spears' "I'm Not a Girl Not Yet a Woman". The line, "don't force me to feel", was inspired by the line, "don't tell me to shut my eyes".

Page 104: Written about my best friend, who has always supported everything I've done with writing, right from the very beginning.

Fun Facts, Part 2: The Journey.

Just a Thought- Freely writing poems with no deadlines or specific goals. Googled "self-publishing" and looked at a few websites over a couple of days. Was discouraged by a) the lack of information and b) the cost of "self-publishing". Requested information about "black and white publishing" from one of the websites I came across. (Xlibris) Two days later I received an email about a great deal/discount they had going, so I jumped at the chance to try and publish my collection of poems. I sent the poems, a quick blurb/bio, and a rough draft for a cover I whipped up on Microsoft Publisher. Xlibris collated the files and sent me back a pdf version of the book, I approved, and the book was published.

Reimagined Moments- After publishing two other books and creating a new look for this updated and cohesive poetry collection, I went back over the original poems from *Just a Thought* with a fine-toothed editing comb. I fixed all the grammatical errors and updated the language to give each poem a fresh new life- saving those that were perfect as they were in their original form. I formatted the entire interior, outsourced a professional cover designer, and added extra bonus content. I used Print on Demand platforms to publish all on my own.

Fun Facts, Part 3: The Dream.

Just a Thought- To try and see if I could publish a book. Out of sheer curiosity. I said if I ever wrote 100 poems, I would give it a try.

Reimagined Moments- To give new life to, and right some wrongs for, *Just a Thought*. To create a beautiful "then and now" piece to reflect how far I've come as a writer and show newbie writers that it's ok to make mistakes- we all grow and learn with time and experience. To add to a new collection of poetry books that will fill shelves over the years to come.

REIMAGINED MOMENTS

ACKNOWLEDGMENTS

This book owes a massive thanks to my amazing CP, Alex Clifford. Alex has read, edited, reread, proofread, critiqued, questioned, supported and all round lifted this book up. I've barely done anything to this book, honestly. It was all her. Her love, her kindness, her feedback, her participation. I swear, every time she thought I was done, I'd ask for her help with "one more thing". (She probably could've rereleased this book without me.)
You're an absolute champion, Alex. I will be forever grateful for your help in righting wrongs and giving this book the love, attention, and new life that it deserves.

I also have to thank my incredible partner. All those years ago he saw something that was worth supporting and has never wavered- even when I have doubted my future as an author, he has always encouraged me to push on and go after my dream.
Brad, you are the reason I get to see my half-assed attempt Reimagined. You are the reason I get to bring new life to this book. Because your support is the life force in every book I write. Because I wouldn't be able to do it without you.
I love you, Babe. Thank you for making all my dreams come true.

ABOUT THE AUTHOR

Jacinta is the author of poetry books, Just a Thought, Emotional Ramblings and When Straight Lines Aren't. Residing in Victoria, Australia, she is a new mother, learning to juggle parenting with her love of writing. She has a blog, on her website, where she shares her experiences as a "newbie" writer and her advice to those who feel the same.

CONNECT WITH JACINTA

www.jacintahudson.com
www.tiktok.com/@jacintahudson3
www.instagram.com/jacintahudson
www.facebook.com/JacintaHudsonWriting

www.ingramcontent.com/pod-product-compliance
Lightning Source LLC
Chambersburg PA
CBHW070307010526
44107CB00056B/2511